Hal•Leonard
BASS
PLAY-ALONG

AUDIO
ACCESS
INCLUDED

PLAYBACK+
Speed • Pitch • Balance • Loop

METALLICA
1991 – 2016

Play 8 Songs with Tab and Sound-alike Audio

CONTENTS

Cover photo © Getty Images / Frank Micelotta

To access audio visit:
www.halleonard.com/mylibrary

Enter Code
3295-9457-7427-1817

ISBN 978-1-4950-9482-8

Hal•LEONARD

Visit Hal Leonard Online at
www.halleonard.com

Contact Us:
Hal Leonard
7777 West Bluemound Road
Milwaukee, WI 53213
Email: info@halleonard.com

In Europe contact:
Hal Leonard Europe Limited
Distribution Centre, Newmarket Road
Bury St Edmunds, Suffolk, IP33 3YB
Email: info@halleonardeurope.com

In Australia contact:
Hal Leonard Australia Pty. Ltd.
4 Lentara Court
Cheltenham, Victoria, 3192 Australia
Email: info@halleonard.com.au

The Day That Never Comes

Music by Metallica
Lyrics by James Hetfield

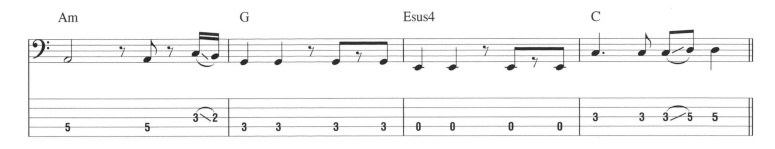

Verse

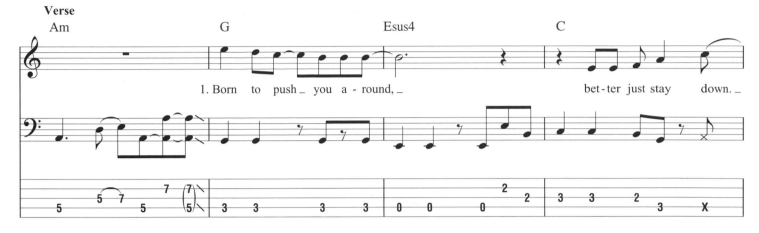

1. Born to push _ you a - round, _   bet - ter just stay   down. _

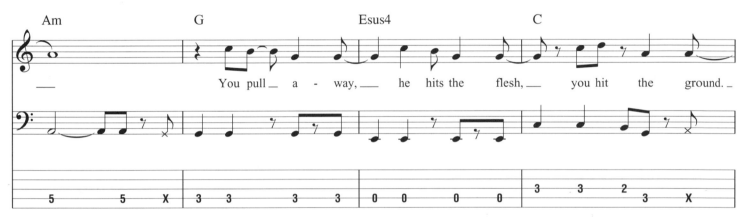

_   You pull _ a - way, _   he hits the   flesh, _   you hit   the   ground. _

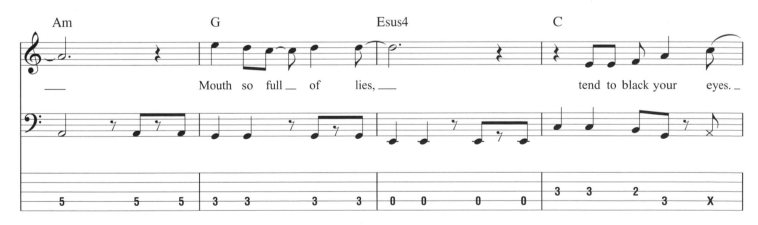

_   Mouth so full _ of   lies, _   tend to black your   eyes. _

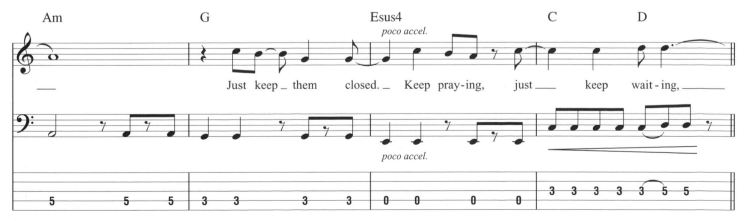

_   Just keep _ them   closed. _ Keep pray - ing,   just _   keep   wait - ing, _

3

§ **Chorus**
Slightly faster ♩ = 124

To Coda ⊕

Slightly slower ♩ = 120

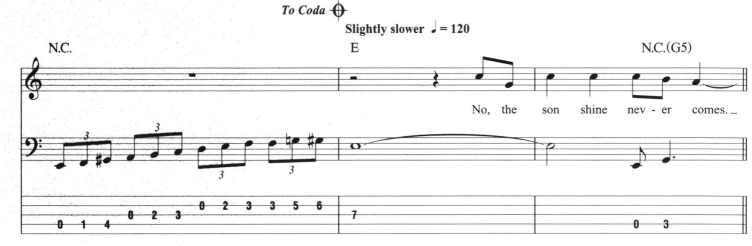

No, the son shine nev - er comes. _

Interlude

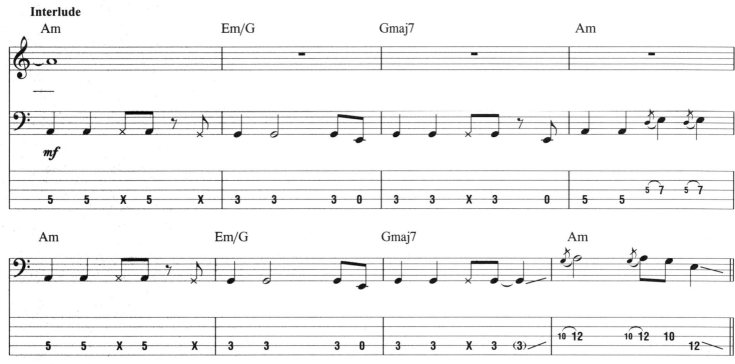

Verse

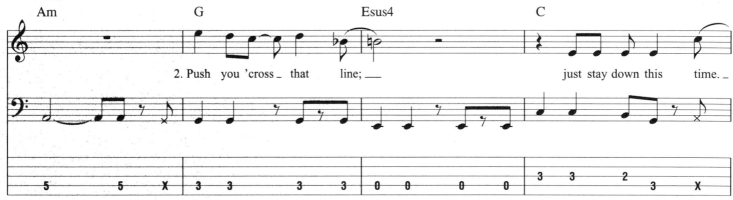

2. Push you 'cross _ that line; _ just stay down this time. _

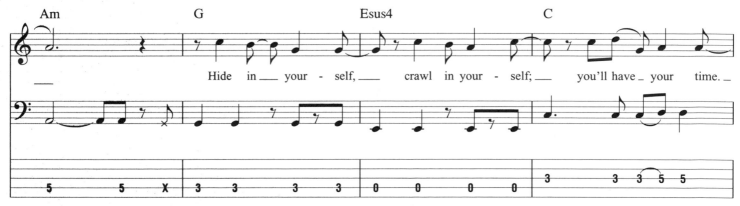

Hide in _ your - self, _ crawl in your - self; _ you'll have _ your time. _

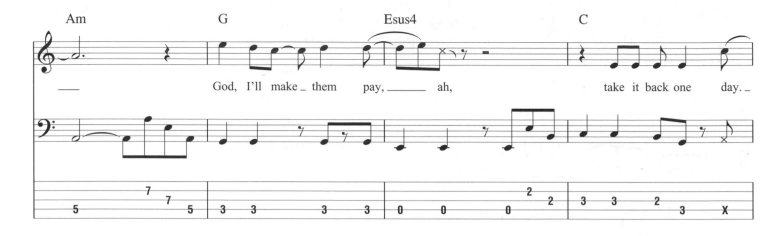

God, I'll make them pay, _____ ah, take it back one day. ___

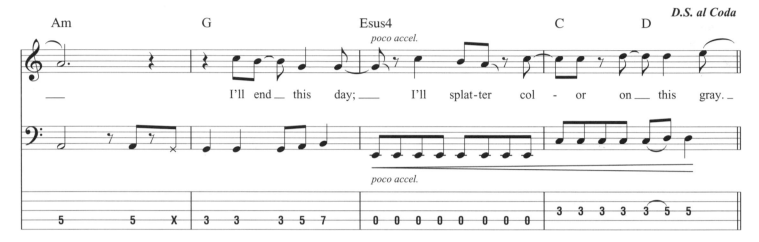

D.S. al Coda

I'll end this day; ____ I'll splat-ter col - or on this gray. __

poco accel.

Coda

Interlude
Faster ♩ = 134

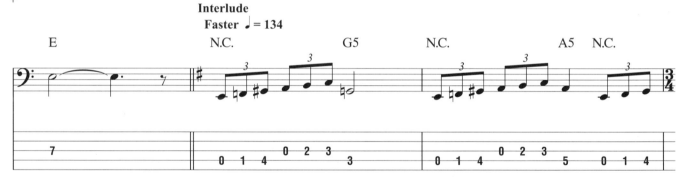

Slightly slower ♩ = 126

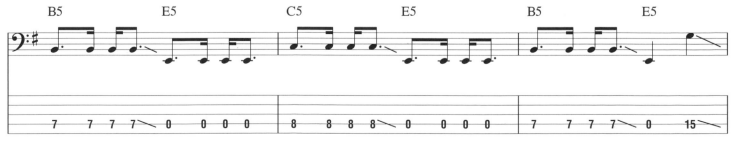

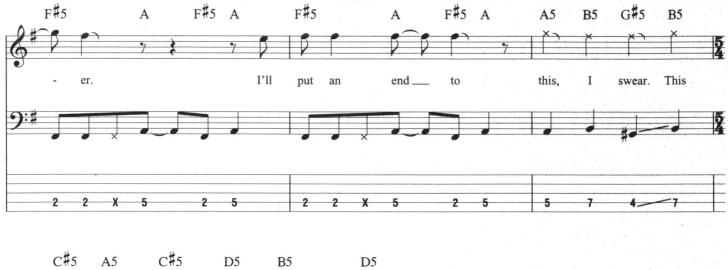

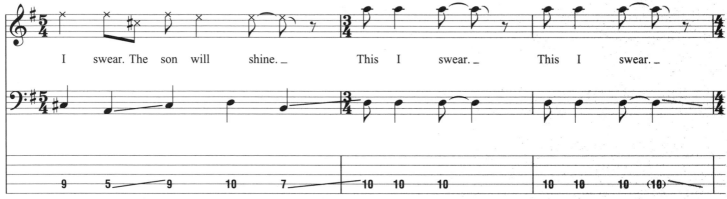

Slightly faster ♩ = 134

Interlude
Very fast ♩ = 264

N.C.(E5)

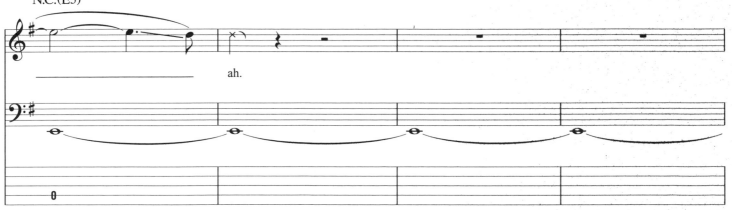

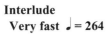

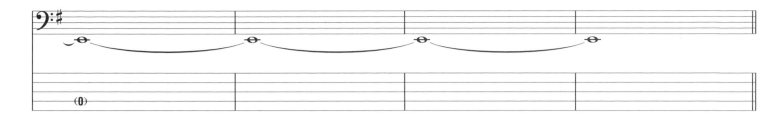

N.C.(E5)

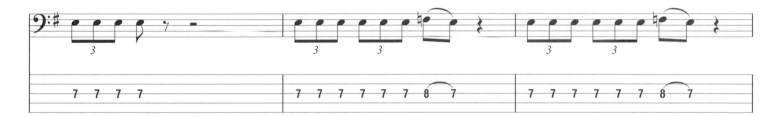

D#5   N.C.(E5)

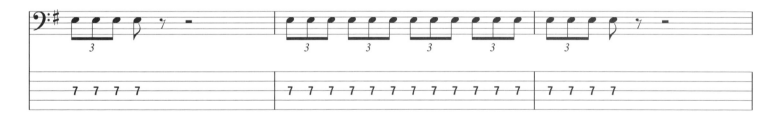

E5   F#5   G5

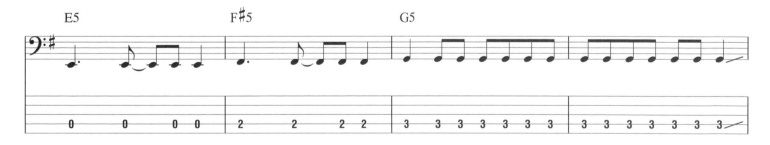

C5   B5   A5   G5

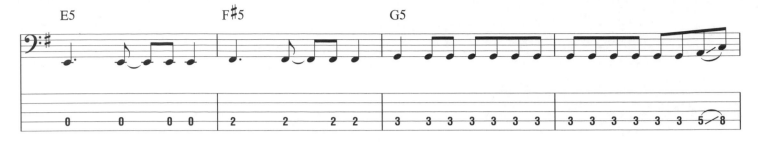

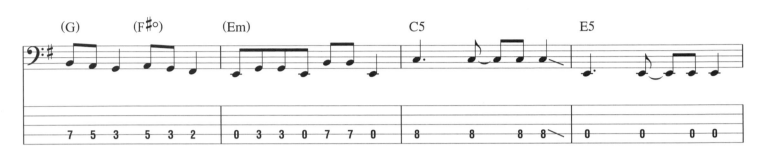

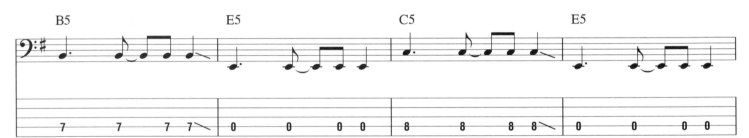

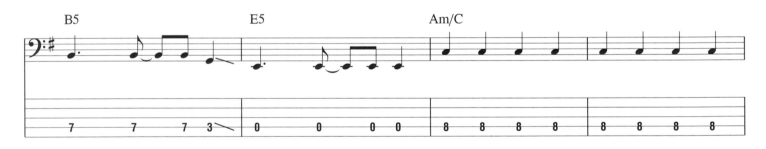

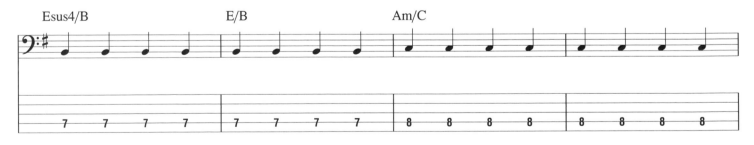

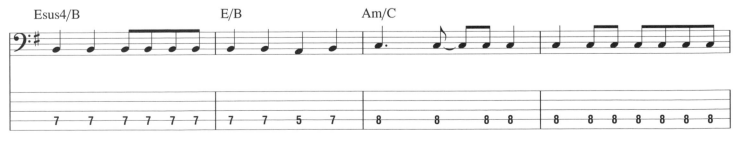

Guitar Solo
Slightly faster ♩ = 268

E5

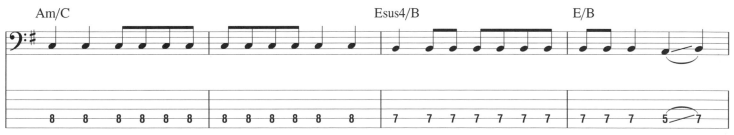

Outro

Am/C   Esus4/B   E/B

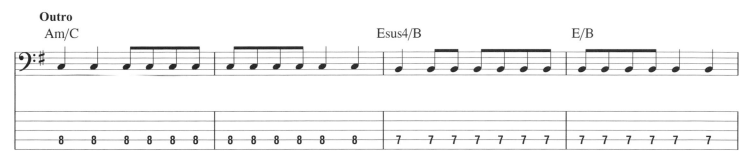

Am/C   Esus4/B   E/B

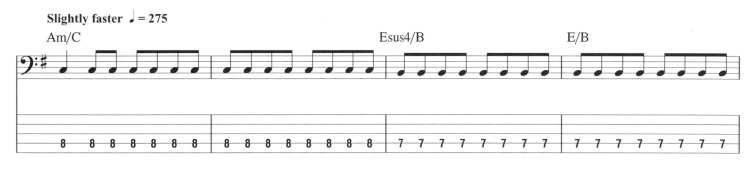

Slightly faster ♩ = 275

Am/C   Esus4/B   E/B

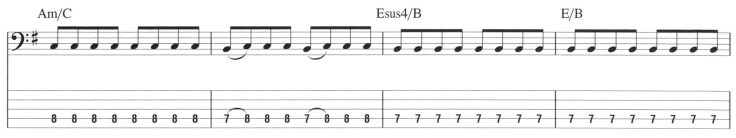

Am/C   Esus4/B   E/B

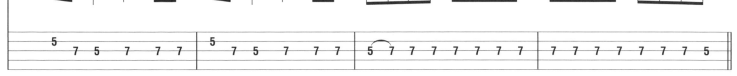

Slightly slower ♩ = 268

C5   E5   B5   E5

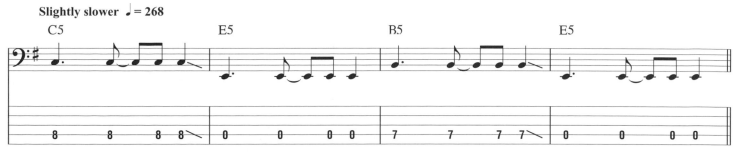

Enter Sandman

Words and Music by James Hetfield, Lars Ulrich and Kirk Hammett

To Coda

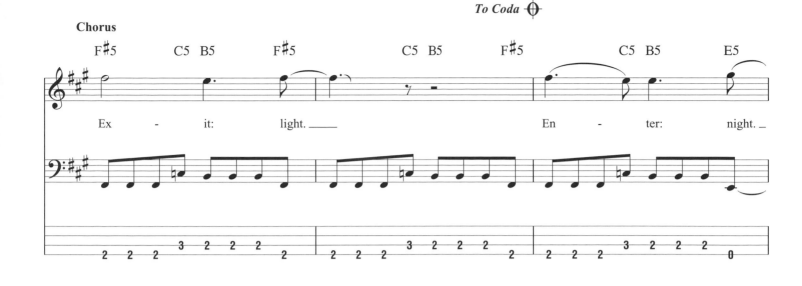

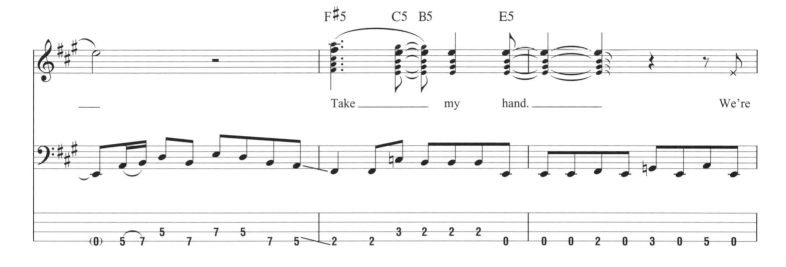

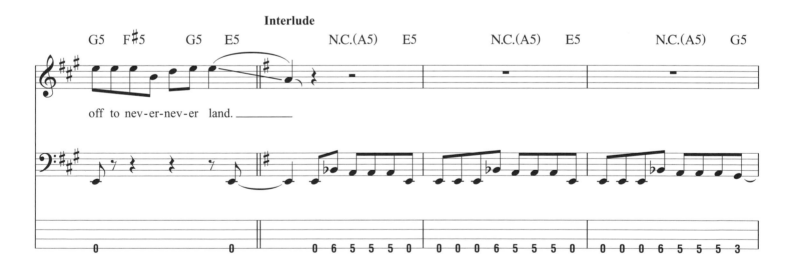

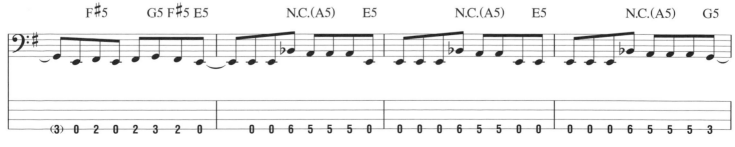

Frantic

Words and Music by James Hetfield, Lars Ulrich, Kirk Hammett and Bob Rock

Drop D tuning, down 1 step:
(low to high) C-G-C-F

Intro
Moderately fast ♩ = 162

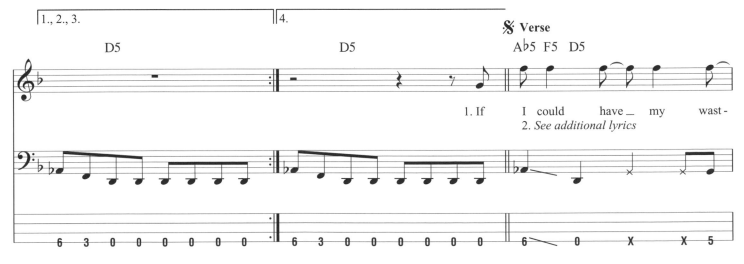

28

*Tune 4th string down 1 step to B♭.

**Performed as open 3rd string
(retuned to F) on original recording.

Additional Lyrics

2. I've worn out always being afraid, an endless stream of fear that I've made.
   Treading water full of worry, this frantic, tick, tick, talk of hurry.
   Do I have the strength to know how I'll go?
   Can I find it inside to deal with what I shouldn't know?
   Worn out always being afraid, an endless stream of fear that I've made.

King Nothing

Words and Music by James Hetfield, Lars Ulrich and Kirk Hammett

Fuel

Words and Music by James Hetfield, Lars Ulrich and Kirk Hammett

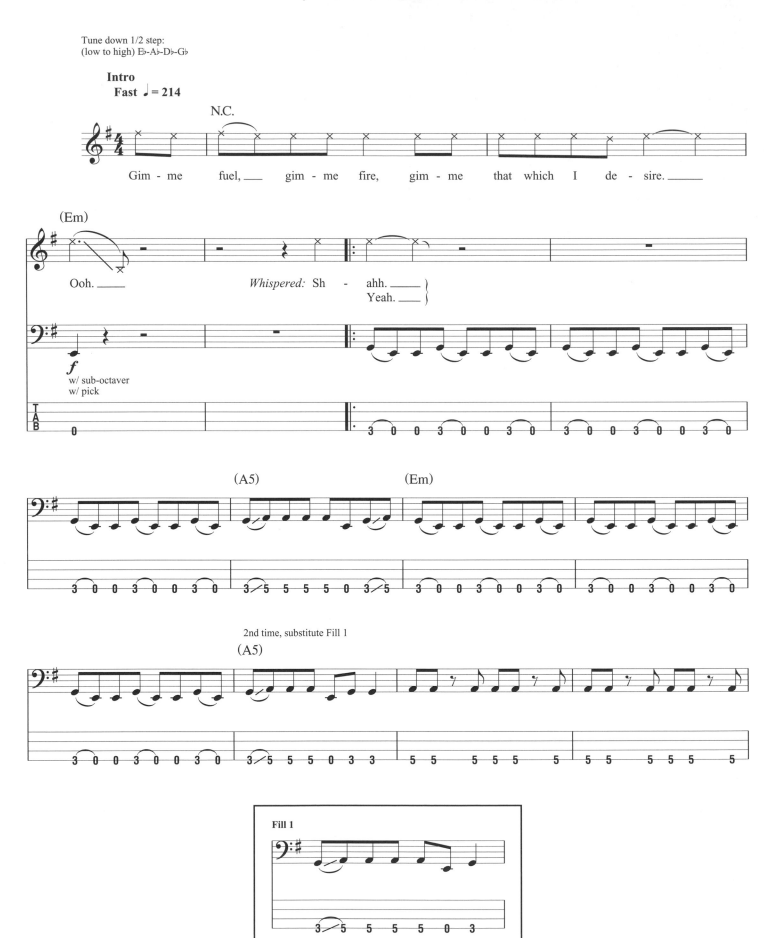

(A7(no3rd)) (C)

churn-ing my di - rec - tion. _____ Quench my

End Voc. Fig. 1

(D) (Em)

thirst with _ gas - o - line. _____ So gim-me

1.
Interlude
N.C.(Em)

E5 N.C.

fuel, _ gim-me fire, gim-me that which I de - sire. _____

2.
Interlude
N.C. A5/E G5 E5

Ooh, _____ yeah, heh. _____

White - knuck - le   tight.

Additional Lyrics

2. Turn on beyond the bone.
   Swallow future, spit out home.
   Burn your face upon the chrome.
   Yeah, oh, yeah.
   Take the corner, join the crash, ah.
   Headlights, (headlines), headlines,
   Another junkie lives too fast.
   Yeah, lives way too fast, (fast), fast, (fast), fast, (fast), whoa.

Moth into Flame

Words and Music by James Hetfield and Lars Ulrich

Verse

N.C.(E5)

1. Blacked out, pop __ queen, am-phet - a - mine. The screams crashed in - to si -

- lence. __ Tapped out, doused __ in the gas - o - line, the

high times go - ing time - less. __ Dec - a - dence, death __

__ of the in - no-cence. The path - way starts to spi - ral. __

In - fa - my all __ for pub-lic - i - ty, de - struc - tion go - ing vi -

duced you in - to ru - in.

flame. _____ Burn!

Interlude

Bb5 E5   G5 A5   Bb5 E5

Play 3 times

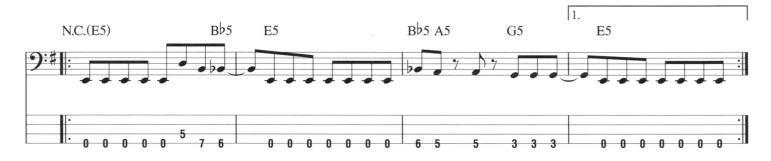

N.C.(E5)   Bb5   E5   Bb5 A5   G5   E5   1.

2.

Bridge

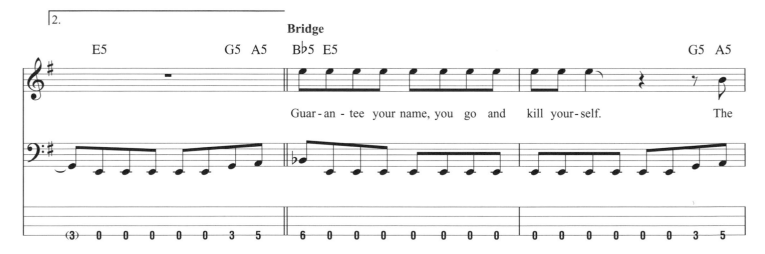

E5   G5 A5   Bb5 E5   G5 A5

Guar - an - tee your name, you go and kill your - self. The

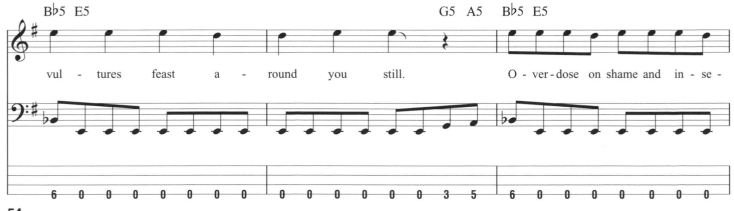

Bb5 E5   G5 A5   Bb5 E5

vul - tures feast a - round you still. O - ver - dose on shame and in - se -

Guitar Solo

*Played 1 octave lower on 5th string (B) on original recording.

*Played 1 octave lower on 5th string on original recording.

Nothing Else Matters

Words and Music by James Hetfield and Lars Ulrich

1. So close no mat-ter how far. Could-n't be much more
2., 3. *See additional lyrics*

from the heart. For-ev-er trust-ing who we are,

and noth-ing else mat-ters.

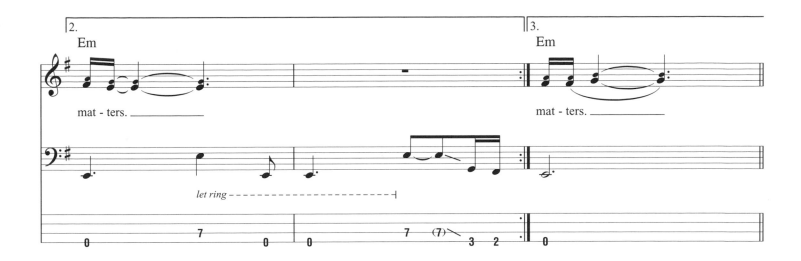

Chorus

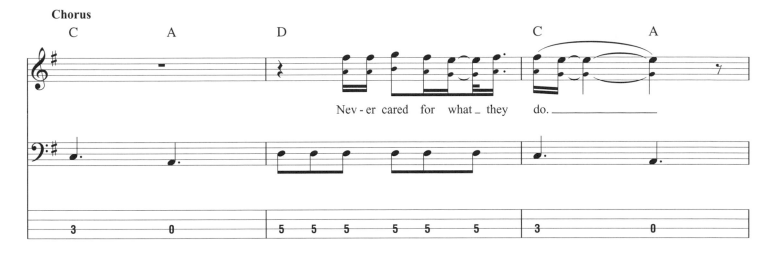

Nev - er cared for what they do.

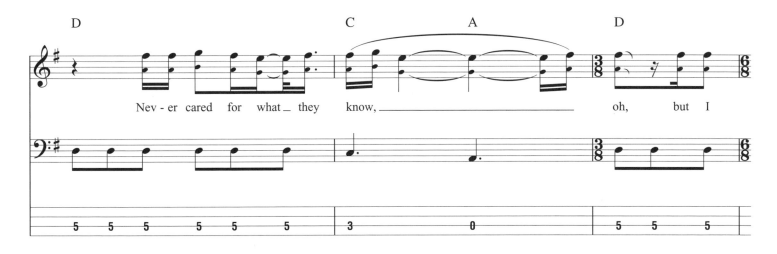

Nev - er cared for what they know, oh, but I

Verse

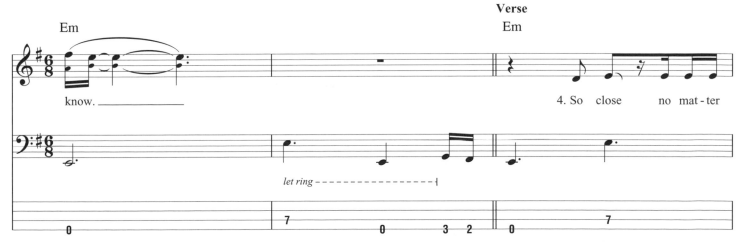

know. 4. So close no mat - ter

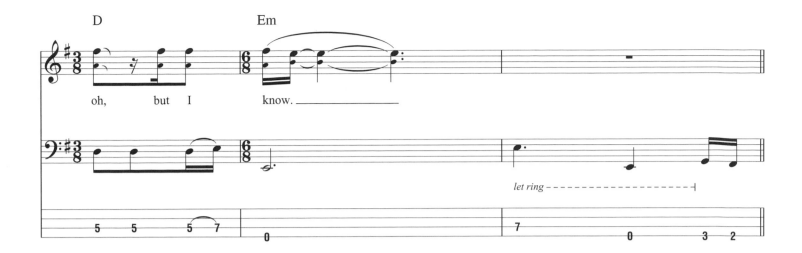

oh,   but I   know.

Interlude

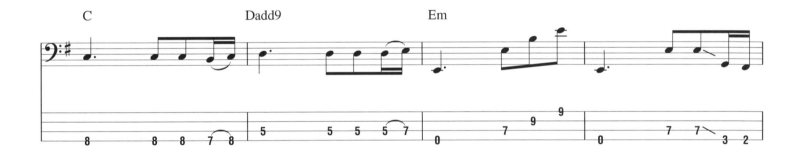

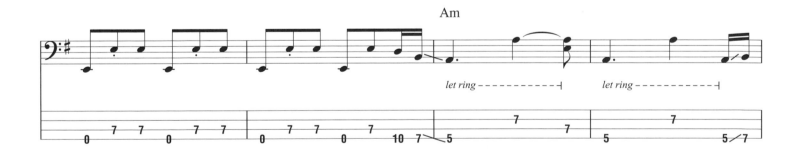

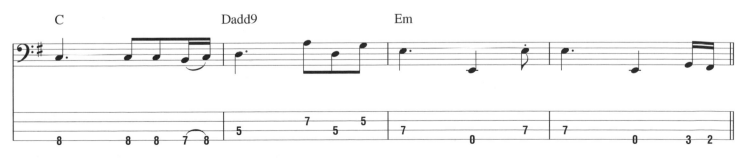

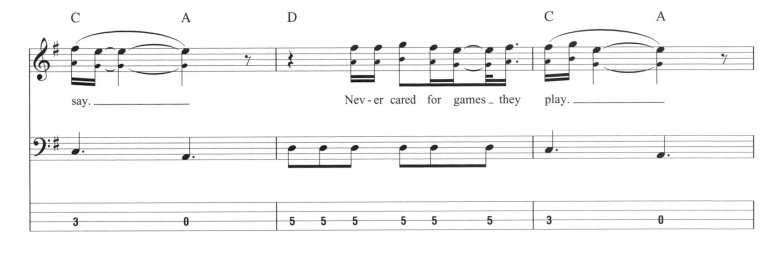

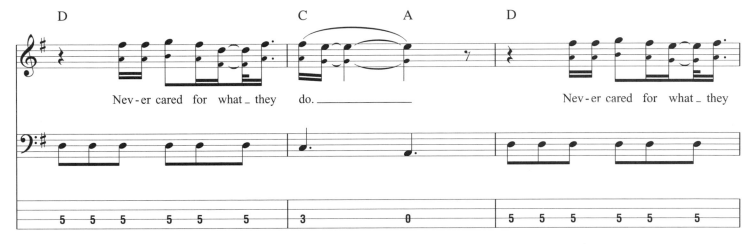

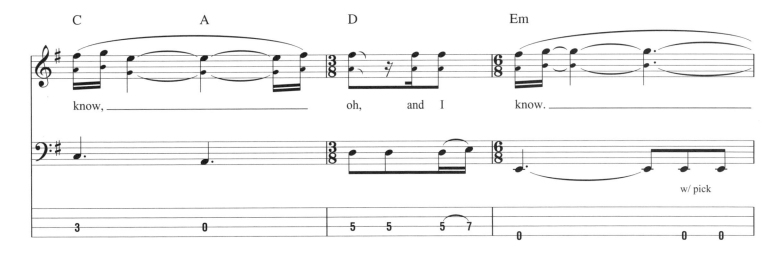

Guitar Solo

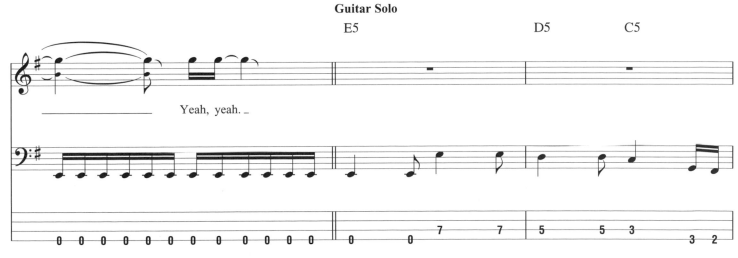

Additional Lyrics

2. Never opened myself this way.
   Life is ours; we live it our way.
   All these words I don't just say,
   And nothing else matters.

3., 6. Trust I seek and I find in you.
   Ev'ry day for us, something new.
   Open mind for a diff'rent view,
   And nothing else matters.

The Unforgiven

Words and Music by James Hetfield, Lars Ulrich and Kirk Hammett

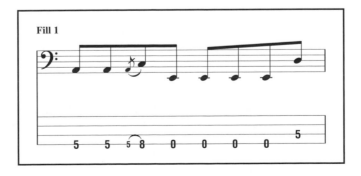

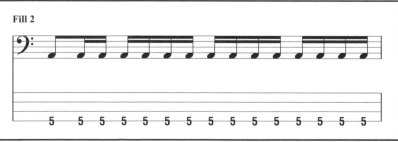

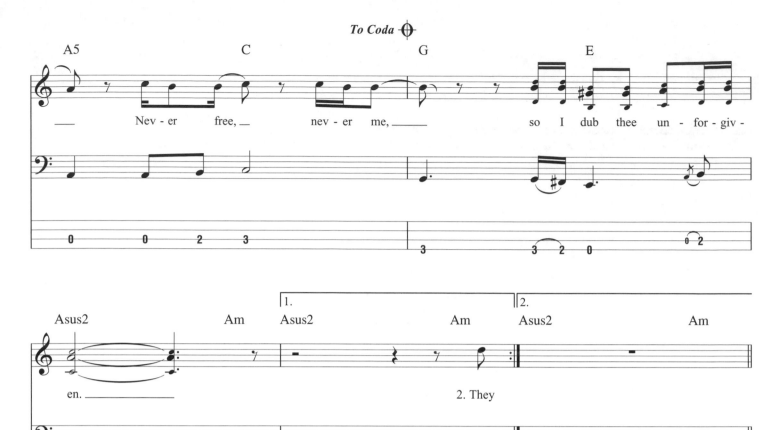

Nev - er free, ___ nev - er me, ___ so I dub thee un - for - giv-

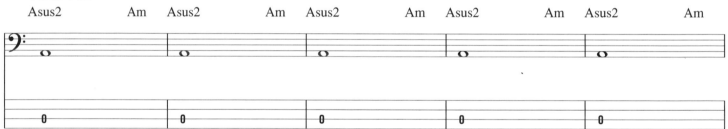

en. ___

2. They

Guitar Solo

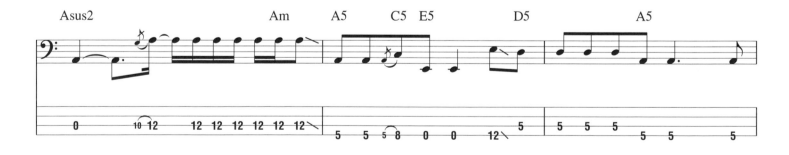

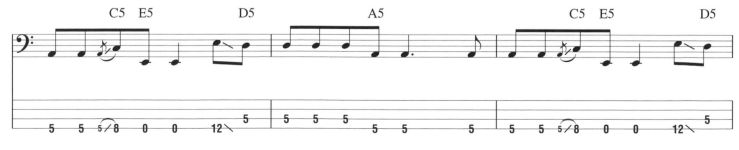

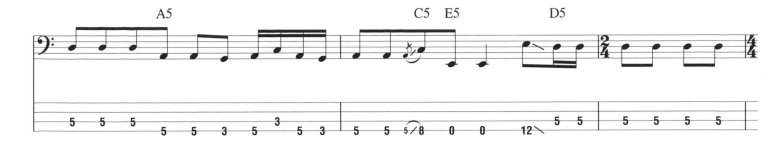

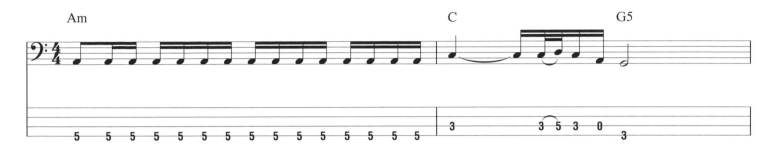

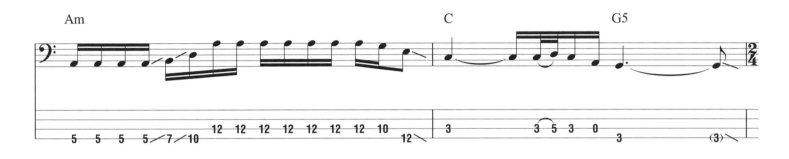

D.S. al Coda

Coda

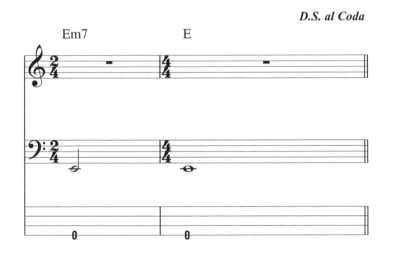

so I dub thee un-for-giv-

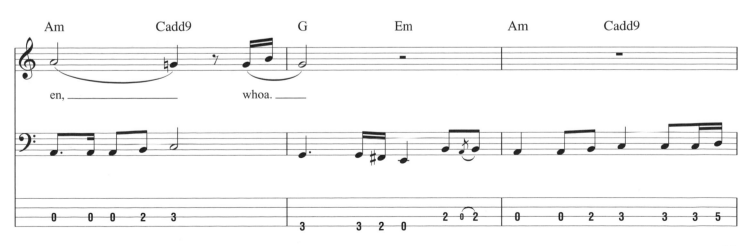

en, _____ whoa. _____

Outro-Chorus

You la-beled me.___ I'll la-bel you.___ So I dub thee un-for-giv-

en.___ Nev-er free,_ nev-er me._

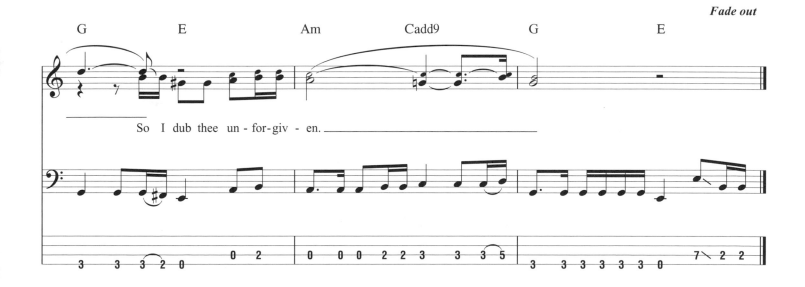

So I dub thee un-for-giv - en.___

Additional Lyrics

2. They dedicate their lives to running all of his.
He tries to please them all, this bitter man he is.
Throughout his life the same, he's battled constantly.
This fight he cannot win, a tired man they see no longer cares.
The old man then prepares to die regretfully.
That old man here is me.

BASS NOTATION LEGEND

Bass music can be notated two different ways: on a *musical staff*, and in *tablature*

THE MUSICAL STAFF shows pitches and rhythms and is divided by bar lines into measures. Pitches are named after the first seven letters of the alphabet.

TABLATURE graphically represents the bass fingerboard. Each horizontal line represents a string, and each number represents a fret.

Notes:

Strings:

3rd string, open   2nd string, 2nd fret   1st & 2nd strings open, played together

---

HAMMER-ON: Strike the first (lower) note with one finger, then sound the higher note (on the same string) with another finger by fretting it without picking.

PULL-OFF: Place both fingers on the notes to be sounded. Strike the first note and without picking, pull the finger off to sound the second (lower) note.

LEGATO SLIDE: Strike the first note and then slide the same fret-hand finger up or down to the second note. The second note is not struck.

SHIFT SLIDE: Same as legato slide, except the second note is struck.

TRILL: Very rapidly alternate between the notes indicated by continuously hammering on and pulling off.

TREMOLO PICKING: The note is picked as rapidly and continuously as possible.

VIBRATO: The string is vibrated by rapidly bending and releasing the note with the fretting hand.

SHAKE: Using one finger, rapidly alternate between two notes on one string by sliding either a half-step above or below.

NATURAL HARMONIC: Strike the note while the fret hand lightly touches the string directly over the fret indicated.

MUFFLED STRINGS: A percussive sound is produced by laying the fret hand across the string(s) without depressing them and striking them with the pick hand.

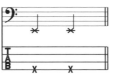

BEND: Strike the note and bend up the interval shown.

BEND AND RELEASE: Strike the note and bend up as indicated, then release back to the original note. Only the first note is struck.

RIGHT-HAND TAP: Hammer ("tap") the fret indicated with the "pick-hand" index or middle finger and pull off to the note fretted by the fret hand.

LEFT-HAND TAP: Hammer ("tap") the fret indicated with the "fret-hand" index or middle finger.

SLAP: Strike ("slap") string with right-hand thumb.

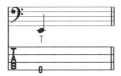

POP: Snap ("pop") string with right-hand index or middle finger.

Additional Musical Definitions

 (accent) • Accentuate note (play it louder)

 (accent) • Accentuate note with great intensity

 (staccato) • Play the note short

D.S. al Coda • Go back to the sign (𝄋), then play until the measure marked ***"To Coda"***, then skip to the section labelled ***"Coda."***

Fill • Label used to identify a brief pattern which is to be inserted into the arrangement.

 • Repeat measures between signs.

 • When a repeated section has different endings, play the first ending only the first time and the second ending only the second time.